DANIEL

FAR FROM HOME

10 Publishing
a division of 10 of those.com

DANIEL: Far From Home

Published 2012

Published by 10Publishing, a division of 10ofthose.com
Unit 19 Common Bank Industrial Estate, Ackhurst Road, Chorley, PR7 1NH
Email: info@10ofthose.com
Website: www.10ofthose.com

British Library Cataloguing in Publication Data.
A catalogue record for this book is available from the British Library.

ISBN: 978-1-906173-68-5

Cover Design and Typeset by: Diane Bainbridge
Printed by: www.printbridge.co.uk

Justin Mote

40 UNDATED DEVOTIONS THROUGH THE BOOK OF DANIEL

DAY 1

READ Daniel 1:1–7

These verses set the context for the whole book. They also introduce us to some of its big themes. Verse 1 tells us that we are in the early years of the sixth century BC. God's people, Israel, had split into two kingdoms after the reign of Solomon. The larger, northern kingdom, retaining the name Israel, had been destroyed 140 years earlier. The southern kingdom, Judah, survived longer. But now it was under siege from the king of the then world superpower, Babylon.

Although Babylon versus Judah was no contest, verse 2 tells us that the Lord delivered the king of Judah into Nebuchadnezzar's hands. The reason for this is explained in 2 Kings 24 and 2 Chronicles 36. There we learn that the king and the people rejected the Lord, and refused to listen to the warnings of the prophets.

Verse 2 is therefore telling us that the defeat of Judah and the removal of articles from the Temple (which was also destroyed by the Babylonians) was the judgement of God on Judah. It also shows us that while Nebuchadnezzar was king of the Babylonians, God was the one who ultimately ruled.

It wasn't just articles from the Temple that were taken to Babylon. In verses 3 to 7 a particular group from Judah are exiled into Babylon. It was a brilliant strategy by Nebuchadnezzar. He exiled anyone who might lead a rebellion against him, and he sought to turn them into Babylonians. His state-funded, three-year course at the University of Babylon would fill the exiles' stomachs with the food of Babylon and their minds with the culture of Babylon so that they would become Babylonians.

Among the exiles are four men who feature throughout the rest of the book, found in verses 6 and 7. These four represent the many who are exiled to Babylon. They are placed in a strange pagan land that seeks to make them just like the Babylonian world around them. Just as Adam and Eve were exiled from the Garden of Eden as a result of their sin, so Judah is exiled from her land as a result of her sin.

The situation for these exiles is similar to ours. The apostle Peter describes us as aliens and strangers in this world (1 Pet. 2:11). The apostle Paul tells us that we are citizens of heaven (Phil. 3:20). We live in a world that seeks to make us conform to its ways (Rom. 12:2). The pressures to compromise that the exiles are about to face are similar to the pressures we face, too.

REFLECTION

Why is it that we forget that we are exiles in this world? What impact do you think it would make if we were more conscious of our real home being heaven?

DAY 2

READ Daniel 1:8–14

In verses 1 to 7 we have seen that Daniel and his friends are living in a strange land. We see them learning the language and the literature of Babylon (v. 4). Furthermore, they received new Babylonian names (v. 7). In other words, these four men engaged with the world in which God had placed them.

However, being part of the world can only go so far. There is a point where cooperation becomes compromise. And for Daniel we see that in verse 8.

There has been much debate as to why Daniel saw this as the line not to cross. It is unlikely that the issue is over the food laws of Leviticus 11. More probable is that Daniel knew the prophecy of Isaiah. Isaiah, centuries earlier, had warned the people of Jerusalem of God's judgement. Judgement from God should have been marked by mourning (see Isa. 22:12,13), though in fact he says that people will 'eat and drink… for tomorrow we die'. The exile was the judgement of God at Judah's sin. This was a time for mourning, nor feasting.

Daniel knew that instead of eating and drinking from the king's table, he should not 'defile' himself. The word 'defile' means Daniel knew that to eat and drink the king's food and wine would make him unclean in God's sight. It would be sin.

Notice (v. 8) that Daniel doesn't just 'resolve'. Resolve without action is just good intention!

In verses 9 and 10 we see that God (who we have already seen is in control, v. 2) causes the official to show favour to Daniel, despite his fear of the king. We are allowed to see behind the scenes here and learn that God is at work. Daniel doesn't know this at this point.

The resolve of verse 8 is accompanied by the action that Daniel takes in verses 11 to 14. He asks the official to allow the exiles a ten-day vegan diet. Daniel appears confident that the Lord will cause those who stand firm for Him to be vindicated. His resolve and action could have had awful consequences. But placed in a strange land, here we see Daniel is determined to stand firm in obedience to God's word.

In the book of Daniel we will see the exiles under pressure to break God's law (e.g. in chapters 3 and 6). In those situations, standing for God rather than going along with the world would result in a death penalty. Might it be that Daniel was able to stand out and obey God's word later because he had resolved to stand out for God right from the start? Might it be that standing out and obeying God's word on a seemingly 'small' issue made it easier to stand out on issues of life and death later?

REFLECTION

God wants us to stand for Him in the world. How do we learn the line between involvement in the world and compromise with the world?

DAY 3

READ Daniel 1:15–21

We have seen that placed in a strange land, Daniel and his three friends are determined to live under God's word in exile. It has led them to a ten-day vegan diet. The result, in verse 15, is that they look better nourished than the rest, and they are allowed to continue to abstain from the king's food.

We are meant to see this as God's miraculous provision. We have already seen God's hand at work for the exiles (see v. 9), and here God is vindicating the exiles' stand for Him. Even in exile, God is in control for the benefit of His people.

In verse 17 we see that the Lord is providing for future events. The exiles are given knowledge and understanding that will mean that they can serve in Babylon. Further, Daniel is given the ability to interpret dreams. In a future chapter we will see that this ability will cause God's people to be rescued from death, and cause Nebuchadnezzar to come to understand the gospel. Once again we see that God is in complete control.

There is no promise here that if we live in obedience to God's word, things will go well for us in this life. Here we learn that as we are to trust God is in control we live in the world.

In verses 18 to 20 the four exiles are examined by the king. They pass their viva, and are shown to be the top students. Again we see that God's hand is at work in the lives of Daniel and his friends.

The writer adds an important comment for us in verse 21. Daniel remains there until the first year of King Cyrus. It was in that year (see Ezra 1:1) that the exiles were allowed to return to Jerusalem. So we know that Daniel will live through the seventy years of exile.

We will see Daniel continuing to stand firm for the Lord, obedient to His word right through the exile period. His faithfulness will be seen even when he is threatened with death (in chapter 6). Faithfulness on what appear less significant issues (like food and drink here in chapter 1) builds towards faithfulness on what appear bigger issues (like the idolatry of chapter 6).

REFLECTION

What are the seemingly trivial issues where you face pressure to conform to the world?

DAY 4

READ Daniel 2:1–18

The text of Daniel chapters 2 to 7 is written in Aramaic, the language of Babylon. These chapters form a unit within the whole book, and were perhaps to be read by Babylonians as well as God's people. The application of the main ideas is certainly pertinent to those who are not the people of God as well as those who are.

In verses 1 to 3 we read of Nebuchadnezzar troubled and unable to sleep because of a dream. The mention of it being his second year as king (when we know from chapter 1 that he has been king throughout the exiles' three-year training) could either mean the second year since the events of chapter 1, or mean a dream that has troubled the king for many years. He calls in his government department and tells them his problem.

In verses 4 to 6 the astrologers ask for the content of the dream. But Nebuchadnezzar is either crafty or paranoid. How can he be sure that their interpretation isn't just made up? So he asks them to tell him both the content of the dream and its interpretation.

The king offers them both carrot and stick. First the stick in verse 5, with the threat of death. And then in verse 6, the rewards. But in verse 7 the astrologers again ask to know the content of the dream. And again in verses 8 and 9 the king repeats his demands.

Verses 10 and 11 are the heart of the issue. It is repeated twice, so that we don't miss the emphasis: 'There is not a man' (v. 10); 'No one can reveal' (v. 11). To tell the king what he has dreamt is beyond human possibility. The pagan astrologers recognize that this is something only 'the gods' can do (v. 11). Nebuchadnezzar may be the superpower of the superpower, but there are things that are beyond him.

Humankind doesn't know everything and can't do everything. And that ought to humble us. But it doesn't the king of Babylon! In verses 12 and 13 he is enraged and orders the execution of a whole government department. And it means that Daniel and his friends are going to be put to death. If they represent the people of God in exile, then it seems that this could be the end for God's people. And if that happens then the great promises that God has made to Abraham (Gen. 12) and to David (2 Sam. 7) will be unfulfilled.

When Daniel hears of the order, in verse 14, we are told that he speaks with 'wisdom and tact'. Living wisely in a pagan world is something that we should always demonstrate (see Matt. 10:16). It leads Daniel to ask for time to interpret the dream (v. 16).

In verses 17 to 18 Daniel explains the matter to his friends and urges them to pray. Here is Daniel acknowledging dependence on God for mercy not to die at the king's hands. Here is acknowledgment that God can do what no person can do. This is faith.

REFLECTION

Can you think of times when situations have arisen that make it look like God's promises to you won't be fulfilled? How do you respond?

DAY 5

READ Daniel 2:17–23

Chapter 2 has opened with Nebuchadnezzar having a troubling dream that no one can interpret. The death penalty awaits the king's advisers. This includes Daniel and his three friends.

In verse 17 we saw Daniel explain this situation to his friends, and urge them to plead for mercy (v. 18) so that they would not be executed. In the book, Daniel and his friends (who are called by their Jewish names in this chapter) represent God's people in exile. If the king carries through with his threat, it seems that the promises of God made earlier to Abraham and David will not be fulfilled.

The issue that faces the exiles leads them to respond in prayer. In verse 19 we see the answer to the prayer. The Lord reveals the mystery of the dream to Daniel. In a situation that threatens the lives of the exiles and threatens, therefore, the fulfilment of the promises of God, we see that God is in complete control.

The revelation of the mystery leads Daniel to praise in verses 20 to 23. Daniel moves from the general to the specific. He first acknowledges the eternal nature of praise for God. He is worthy of praise for ever and ever. Daniel acknowledges that God has wisdom and power. The Lord stands in contrast to Nebuchadnezzar. He thinks that he has power, but doesn't have the wisdom to understand his dream.

In verses 21 to 22 Daniel continues to expound on the character of God. He is sovereign over nature and sovereign over human rule. Further, wisdom and knowledge are His to give. He knows what people do not.

There is a shift in the praise in verse 23. Daniel's praise becomes personal. He acknowledges God's faithfulness – He is the God of his fathers. This God has given Daniel wisdom and power. It is He who has made known to Daniel the king's dream. God has answered the prayer of the exiles and will, therefore, be faithful to His promises.

Here we see the sovereignty of God and the responsibility of His people working together. God is the one in total control, the one who, alone, can reveal the mystery of the king's dream. And yet we see God's people responding to the threat from the king in prayer.

REFLECTION

Real faith means that we believe that God is the one in complete control of all that happens in our world. Real faith also means that we pray for God to fulfil His promises for His people.

DAY 6

READ Daniel 2:24–49

Verses 24 to 26 describe how Daniel comes before the king. Daniel's first words to the king, verses 27 to 28, are to acknowledge that the God of heaven can reveal mysteries and to tell the king that his dream is a revelation from God. The revelation is about the future (vv. 29,30).

Daniel then tells the king the content of the dream (vv. 31–35). The king has seen a huge statue in five parts. The head, chest, belly, and legs are made of gold, silver, bronze, and iron, with the feet finally a mixture of iron and clay. A rock then strikes the feet of the statue and destroys it, with the rock becoming a mountain that fills the earth.

In verses 36 to 45 Daniel gives the interpretation of the dream to the king. The golden head is Nebuchadnezzar. With echoes of Genesis 1, the king is told that he only has rule in the world because God has given it to him (compare v. 38 with Gen. 1:28).

Nebuchadnezzar's kingdom, however, won't last. We are not told here the identities of the kingdom that will replace it (we are given some clues in later chapters). What is emphasized is that all the kingdoms of this world will end. They will be replaced by a kingdom established by the God of heaven. And that kingdom will endure for ever (v. 44).

At first sight it seems that the king responds in the right way to the interpretation of the dream (vv. 46–49). He states that Daniel's God is the 'Lord of kings', and promotes the exiles in the government. However, we will see that the king is not yet converted.

Nebuchadnezzar has, however, heard the gospel. That God will establish a kingdom is the good news that Jesus also preached (see Mark 1:14,15). This is the message that the pagan world needs to hear. We will see, however, that the king has not yet learned to repent in response to the gospel.

The message of this dream is also a reassurance to the exiles. While their present situation may look as if Nebuchadnezzar is the one in charge and that he rules over God's people, the exiles are being assured that the promises of an eternal kingdom, made centuries earlier to King David (see 2 Sam. 7), will still be fulfilled. God's kingdom will be established.

We know that Jesus is the King who will rule that kingdom. We still pray 'your kingdom come'.

REFLECTION

What Daniel tells the king of Babylon is the gospel. This is the news that the world needs to hear. How involved are you in making this news known to your neighbours, friends and colleagues?

DAY 7

READ Daniel 3:1–7

In chapter 2 we read how Daniel, an exile in a strange land, brought the gospel of God's coming kingdom to the king of Babylon. What Daniel did is what we are called to do as we live as exiles in this world (see Matt. 28:19,20).

The king's response seemed promising (2:47). However, chapter 3 opens with Nebuchadnezzar refusing to live in proper response to the dream he has just had. Instead of worshipping the God of heaven, he establishes an idol that he commands all to bow down to. The repetition of language makes it clear. This is Nebuchadnezzar thinking he is in charge! Four times in these seven verses we are told that this was a statue Nebuchadnezzar had 'set up'.

We are meant to see the irony of this chapter following the dream of chapter 2. In the dream, only the head of the statue was gold. Nebuchadnezzar sets up a statue that is all gold. It is an act in defiant rejection of the dream.

Further, this statue is set up on the 'plain' of Dura. There are similarities to the tower of Babel (see Gen. 11). This is a statue to be seen from a great distance. Here is something that all Babylon can unite around. The universal language of verse 7 is striking.

When the Lord made His promises to Abraham, it would be through his descendants that blessing would come to all nations. Here the king of Babylon is calling all nations to unite around his idol. This proud rejection of what God has revealed to him is but a shadow of how all humankind rejects God.

This is, however, no game of musical statues. The king commands everyone to worship the idol. Disobedience will, v. 6, be serious. It is either bow or burn.

The king's edict isn't preventing people from worshipping their own gods. They do, however, have to acknowledge his god. The exiles know they are not to worship any other god (Exod. 20:1–3). To obey the king's order will mean breaking the first two of the Ten Commandments. But not to worship the king's statue is to suggest that his 'god' is not as equally god as 'Yahweh'. That could appear bigoted and intolerant. The pressure the exiles face – to accept the world's 'gods' as equals with the Lord – is the pressure that we face, too.

The arrogant law of the king is another threat to the existence of God's people, and therefore to the promises of God. If the exiles stand against the king, they will all die in the furnace.

REFLECTION

How do we come under pressure to compromise on the exclusive claims of the Lord and the gospel? What consequences might there be for us when we refuse to accept the 'gods' of other religions, including secularism?

DAY 8

READ Daniel 3:8–18

Chapter 3 has introduced us to the first of the two ways the world seeks to conform us to itself. The exiles are under pressure to conform to the world by doing what God forbids. They are under intense pressure to bow down and worship the statue that King Nebuchadnezzar set up. (We will see the second pressure in chapter 6.)

In verses 8 to 12 we see that officials in Babylon report to the king that Shadrach, Meshach and Abednego are disobeying the king's order. Not only does the pagan world seek to get the exiles to conform to its ways, but it is also opposed to God's people. There is no mention of Daniel in this chapter. It may well be that at this time he is serving in some other part of the Babylonian empire.

The exiles are brought before a furious king (v. 13). He first enquires whether the accusation is true (v. 14), and then gives them the opportunity to conform to his order. Failure to conform will mean certain death (v. 15).

Verses 16 to 18 are wonderful! The exiles are respectful in the way that they answer the king. In verse 17 we see two things. First we see the exiles' confidence in the power of God. They trust that the God they serve 'is able to save us'. They are confident that 'he will rescue us from [the king's] hand'.

Verse 18 begins with a 'but'. The exiles do believe that the Lord will rescue them. However, even if God does not rescue them, they will still not bow down and worship the image of gold. It seems that they believe that if God doesn't rescue them from the furnace, He must have some other way of keeping His promises. They believe that the Lord will be faithful to the promises that He has made.

Faith believes that God keeps His promises. We don't have to compromise with the world to enable Him to do it! Quite the contrary. We believe that God keeps His word, so we should obey Him, even when that obedience makes us think He can't fulfil what He has promised.

REFLECTION

In what ways are you under pressure to do the things that God has forbidden? When is it hard to trust that God will keep His promises to us if we obey Him?

DAY 9

READ Daniel 3:19–30

Shadrach, Meshach and Abednego have not obeyed the king's order. They have not given in to the pressure to do what God forbids. And, respectfully, they have explained to the king their trust in the power and promises of God.

Nebuchadnezzar is furious. People did not disobey him and get away with it. He orders the furnace temperature to be increased. The exiles are tied up in their clothing and thrown in. So hot was it that the soldiers who threw them in were killed.

Verse 24 begins the surprising turn-around of the chapter. The king is astonished. He questions what he sees. In verse 25 we read the report. He has thrown three into the furnace. But now he sees four. He has thrown them to death. But now he sees them alive. He has had them bound and thrown into the fire. But now he sees them unbound and walking.

The exiles' trust has been vindicated (v.17). Back in verse 15 the king thought that he was in control. He boastfully declared, '...what god will be able to rescue you from my hand'. Now he has seen that there is a God bigger than him!

In verse 26 the exiles are commanded out of the fire. The miraculous nature of their escape is underlined in verse 27. There is not even the smell of fire on them.

As we saw at the end of chapter 2, it seems in verses 28 to 30 the king of Babylon has understood the God of the Jews is in control. He praises Him, and confirms the exiles' trust in Him. He then orders that blasphemy against the Lord be punished by death (v. 29), and promotes the three (v. 30). However, as encouraging as this seems, none of these things means that the king is converted. Chapter 4 will show us that.

The exiles are spared the death penalty as they serve God in this distant land. However, we should not read this episode as a promise to us in this life. Hebrews 11:34 alludes to Daniel chapter 3. It tells us that the exiles have demonstrated faith and were rescued. But the chapter continues by telling us that others were not rescued. They 'were put to death by the sword' (v. 37). Faithfulness to the Lord does not guarantee rescue in this world. However, as Hebrews encourages us, faithfulness to the Lord may lead us to suffer now, but will lead us to the ultimate 'rescue' of glory itself.

REFLECTION

What might help you remember that the Lord is the one who is in total control for His people and His promises, and so be encouraged to stand in obedience to Him?

DAY 10

READ Daniel 4:1–18

Chapter 4 starts with a letter or document written by King Nebuchadnezzar. The first and last sections of the chapter are written in the first person, with the middle part written in the third person.

The opening verses are stunning. The king writes his letter to the whole world (v. 1). The phrase 'peoples, nations and men of every language' is familiar to us. We saw back in 3:7 that the phrase was used in the command for people to worship the statue that Nebuchadnezzar had set up. Now the same group is addressed – but not with a command to idolatry, rather with a testimony of a converted man.

In verse 3 we read of the king's declaration about the Most High God. He has come to declare the eternal kingdom of God. He has come to understand what lies at the heart of the gospel.

When the exiles arrived in Babylon, it was the king who wanted them to be assimilated into being Babylonian. But it is through the life and witness of the exiles that the king of Babylon has come to submit to the God of the Jews.

The rest of the chapter details how this happened to Nebuchadnezzar. Once again Nebuchadnezzar had a dream (vv. 4,5 – remember chapter 2). In contrast to before, this time the king tells his advisers the content of the dream, but like before, they were unable to interpret it (vv. 6,7).

In verses 9 to 16 the king tells Daniel the content of the dream. The king has seen a tree that can be seen by all the world. However, as a result of a command from heaven, the tree is to be cut to a stump that is to be bound in iron and bronze. In verse 16 the stump takes on personality. The person is to live with, and like, an animal for seven 'times' or years.

In verse 17 the king is told by the holy messengers that the purpose of his dream was so that people know that Judah's God is the Most High, the true God in control of the kingdoms of this world. The king now wants to know the meaning of the dream (v. 18).

REFLECTION

In this chapter we are seeing how the king has been converted. It reminds us that there is no one too 'hard' for the Lord to humble. Are there people we have stopped praying for because we have forgotten how powerful the Lord and His gospel are?

DAY 11

READ Daniel 4:19–27

Daniel has heard the dream that had troubled Nebuchadnezzar. This next section of the chapter changes back from being told in the first person to the third person. Daniel, troubled by the meaning of the dream, is reassured by the king in verse 19: '...do not let the dream or its meaning alarm you', he says.

First, Daniel identifies the tree as King Nebuchadnezzar. He is a king who has become strong, whose dominion has stretched over distant parts of the world. Indeed, Daniel has positive notes in his description of the king's rule. The tree has provided food and shelter. Babylon isn't just a superpower. It has brought good to others. Similar language of a tree growing large and providing shelter in its branches is used by Jesus when speaking about another kingdom, that of the gospel (see Mark 4:30–32).

In verse 23 Daniel replays verse 16. This becomes the focus of the interpretation that Daniel gives in verses 24 to 27. First, Daniel tells the king the source of the dream. It has come from the Most High God. Further, this dream has been told 'against' the king. He will be driven away from people and will live like an animal for seven years.

The purpose of God doing this to Nebuchadnezzar is so that he will acknowledge that God is sovereign over human kingdoms. Nebuchadnezzar is going to be humbled by the true God. It is only when the king has been humbled by God that his kingdom will be restored to him (v. 27). He must learn that his rule is totally under the rule of God.

Politely Daniel adds verse 27. It is his advice to the king. Daniel instructs the king to repent. Daniel has, therefore, brought the gospel to the king. The gospel is the same in both the Old and New Testaments. It is about learning that God is in control of our world. The gospel is about understanding that we only have anything in this world as a gift from God. The gospel is about being humbled by God.

REFLECTION

The message that Daniel has spoken to the king while in exile is the same as the message that God has given us to speak as we live as exiles in this world. What opportunities have you got to speak this same gospel message? What opportunities could you be praying for?

DAY 12

READ Daniel 4:28–37

Verses 28 to 30 tell of the king's response to the dream, its interpretation and the application from Daniel. We learn that in the year that followed the king hadn't listened and had failed to humble himself before God. As he struts about on the roof of his royal palace, surveying his achievements, the use of the personal pronoun is striking. Despite being repeatedly told that his rule is a gift from God, he still thinks that what he has are his achievements. The king is like so many today.

In verses 31 to 33 we read how the dream the king had was fulfilled. The heavenly messenger repeats the judgement that the king had been told in the dream. And what heaven speaks is what happens (v. 33). The king of the nation that ruled the world is now like a bird. We are not meant to miss the reversal. In his dream Nebuchadnezzar was like a tree that gave sanctuary to birds. Now he has become like one of those birds.

The effect of this judgement from God is the conversion of the king. In verse 34, instead of looking down on what he has achieved, he now looks up to heaven. Humbled by God, he now sees things correctly. He sees his place before the Most High. And it leads the king to a hymn of praise in verses 34 and 35. He now acknowledges the sovereign and eternal God.

C.S. Lewis describes the night he came to the same realization.

> *You must picture me alone in that room in Magdalen, night after night, feeling, whenever my mind lifted even for a second from my work, the steady, unrelenting approach of Him whom I so earnestly desired not to meet. That which I greatly feared had at last come upon me. In the Trinity Term of 1929 I gave in, and admitted that God was God, and knelt and prayed: perhaps, that night, the most dejected and reluctant convert in all England.*[1]

The king's submission to God as the true king is a shadow of the response that all are called to make before King Jesus. As the king submitted to God, his sanity was restored, and now his kingdom is restored too. The last line of the chapter is a summary: '...those who walk in pride he is able to humble.' Jesus taught the same (see Luke 18:14).

REFLECTION

Why do you think it was so hard for Nebuchadnezzar to humble himself before the Lord? Why is it hard for people today to do the same?

DAY 13 Review of Daniel chapters 1 – 4

Some of the main themes of the book of Daniel were introduced in chapter 1. There we saw:

- God is the one in complete control of His world. This is seen in the deliverance of the people of Judah into the hands of the king of Babylon, and in the vindication of His people's stand for Him.
- The people of God are placed in a strange land that seeks to make them conform, so that they are like that world. However, God's people are to stand firm for the Lord, obedient to His word.

As we look back over chapters 2 to 4 we see those themes worked out time and again. We see God's complete control revealed to King Nebuchadnezzar. It is revealed to him in the interpreted dreams that come in both chapters 2 and 4. It is revealed to him in the rescue of Shadrach, Meshach and Abednego in chapter 3.

We have also seen how the exiles live trusting that God is in control. They have learned from the king's dream in chapter 2 that the promises God has made to them through the centuries will still be fulfilled. He will establish a kingdom that will last for ever. The truth of God's sovereignty leads the exiles to stand firmly for God, obedient to His word, even when threatened with death in chapter 3.

Chapter 4 ends with Nebuchadnezzar coming to submit to God's rule. He has, at last, understood the gospel, been humbled by God, and acknowledges God to be the true King. In the historical narrative of the book (chapters 1 – 6), this is the last we read of Nebuchadnezzar. We have traced how he has been changed from tyrannical despot to humble believer. That God can do that, using the courageous stand and bold witness of four young men, is inspiring.

At the start of the book, we might have thought that it was the exiles that would be conformed to the world they were placed in. In reality, it is the king of Babylon who has been conformed – humbled to worship the Most High God.

REFLECTION

How have these chapters helped you be more confident that God is the one in complete control?

How have these chapters encouraged you to live for God in this world?

DAY 14

READ Daniel 5:1–9

Without any explanation, chapter 5 starts with a new king on the throne in Babylon. However, what we have read so far means that we are not surprised that this chapter signals the end of the Babylonian empire (remember the dream in chapter 2, where Nebuchadnezzar was told 'After you, another kingdom will rise', v. 39). In this chapter we will see themes we have met before. A proud king will learn who the real king is.

Verses 1 to 4 describe a banquet hosted by the new king, Belshazzar. The feast is described briefly in verse 1. What the writer draws our attention to (which will later be central to the downfall of the Babylonian empire) is both the idolatry of the king (who praises 'gods of gold and silver, of bronze, iron, wood and stone' and the rejection of Yahweh as God (they deliberately use in their revelry the goblets 'taken from the temple of God in Jerusalem', repeated in both verses 2 and 3).

Belshazzar is wilfully ridiculing the God of the exiles. It stands out after the final words of chapter 4, '...those who walk in pride he [the Lord] is able to humble.'

In verses 5 to 9 we read of the writing on the wall. The phrase has entered our language as a metaphor for disaster or danger being imminent. In verse 5 we read of the fingers of a hand writing on the plaster of the wall. There is no explanation of this here (as there wasn't with the fourth figure in the fiery furnace in chapter 3). Daniel will later explain that this is a hand sent from God (v. 24). (God's finger also brought plagues in Egypt, Exod. 8:19, and the writing of the tablets of the Law, Exod. 31:18.)

It is no surprise that the king turned pale and that his knees started to knock. Belshazzar knows that the words on the wall mean something. His trouble is that he can't understand them. He summons his officials and promises them extraordinary wealth and status if they can interpret the words (v. 7). However, as with Nebuchadnezzar's dreams, there is no one who can tell the king the words' meaning. He is even more frightened.

We are meant to notice the change in the king. In verse 1 he is indulgent and proud. By verse 9 he is powerless and frightened. And this just at the sight of a finger of God!

REFLECTION

Think of a situation where you, or people you know, think too highly of themselves. How do these verses help us, and them, be humble before God?

DAY 15

READ Daniel 5:10–24

No one has been able to interpret the writing on the wall of the banqueting hall in Babylon. However, in verse 10 a woman enters who tells the king not to be alarmed. It is unlikely to be one of Belshazzar's queens – they were present already (v. 2). Most likely this is either Belshazzar's mother, or a wife of Nebuchadnezzar. She is clearly someone who remembers Daniel (vv. 11,12), who now seems to have been out of favour at court (v. 13 suggests that). In verses 11 to 12 we are being given a rerun of chapter 4. The queen advises the king to call for Daniel.

Daniel is brought before the king (v. 13). Twice the king says he has 'heard' about Daniel's wisdom and ability to give interpretations. His own officials cannot explain the writing. Daniel is asked for the meaning, and is promised high status if he can deliver (v. 16).

Daniel's response in verse 17 stands in contrast to his earlier responses to Nebuchadnezzar. Instead of an exhortation to change, Daniel will pronounce judgement.

In verses 18 to 21 Daniel doesn't interpret the writing on the wall. Instead, he gives another summary of the events of chapter 4. That this has happened twice in the section already suggests it is vital for what comes.

Verse 22 begins with a 'but'. Here is a contrast. The contrast is between the response of Nebuchadnezzar in his acknowledgement of the Sovereign God, and that of Belshazzar. Daniel spells it out to the king in verse 22, '...you... have not humbled yourself'. Belshazzar doesn't receive the dreams his father had. He didn't need to know how he should have lived. This king knew the 'gospel' – he knew what had happened to his father. He knew that God was King and that he should live humbly before Him. Belshazzar is just like all people when they reject what they know. (See Rom. 1:18–32.)

God doesn't have to give 'new revelation' in each generation. The writing of what God has done in the past is sufficient.

'Instead', we are told the decision of the king, 'to set [himself] up against the Lord of heaven' (v. 23). And we are told the evidence of that arrogance (vv. 23b,24a). In verse 24 we see the parallel of what it means to be against God. It is to be as Belshazzar who 'did not honour the God who holds in his hand your life'.

REFLECTION

Chapters 4 and 5 (which come right in the middle of the Aramaic section of the book) present us with two ways we can live before God. We can either be humbled by Him or we can stand proudly against Him. Which are we seeking to do?

DAY 16

READ Daniel 5:25–31

In this section we are going to read of the judgement pronounced by God on Belshazzar. However, before reading and interpreting the writing on the wall, we have already read the basis for the judgement (vv. 22–24). Belshazzar's proud rejection of God as King was a rejection of the gospel (revealed in the experience of his father). Twice in chapter 5 we have been reminded of what happened in chapter 4.

In verses 25 to 28 we discover both the words written on the wall, and their significance. The plain meaning of the words would have been understood by those at court. They are written in the Babylonian language of Aramaic. They are three words describing measures of 'weight': Mene, Tekel and Peres (or Parsin).

The word 'Mene' is repeated, adding emphasis to the judgement from God. Belshazzar's days are brought to an end. The reason is explained in the second word, 'Tekel'. In the scales of God's justice, Belshazzar has been weighed and found wanting. The implication of the judgement comes in the third word, 'Peres'. Belshazzar's kingdom is divided and will be given to the Medes and Persians.

In verse 29 we read of Belshazzar's response to the pronouncement of God's judgement. Belshazzar's response is to do what he promised (v. 16), but he fails to listen to what Daniel has said. Belshazzar stands in contrast to the Ninevites, who when hearing a similar message 'repented' (see Jonah 3). Belshazzar stands alongside the religious leaders of Jesus' day. They too heard the pronouncement of God's judgement but continued in rebellion against God (see Mark 12:1–12).

In verses 30 to 31 God's word to Belshazzar is fulfilled. It is not just that Belshazzar is slain, but that the Babylonian kingdom has fallen. God's word to Nebuchadnezzar, through the interpreted dream of chapter 2 (see 2:39), has also been fulfilled. Mighty Babylon has fallen. Kingdoms will come and go, but the word of the Lord stands firm. The Lord God is truly the one who rules in this world.

REFLECTION

The gospel is both the announcement of salvation to those humbled by God, and judgement to those who remain in defiant rejection of Him. This is the gospel spoken by Daniel and the exiles in Babylon. This is the gospel we speak to our world.

DAY 17

READ Daniel 6:1–9

At the end of chapter 5 we saw the great Babylonian kingdom defeated and replaced by the Persians. King Darius is the new superpower.

In Daniel 6:1–3, the focus is on Daniel's position in the new kingdom. It appears in chapter 5 that during the reign of Belshazzar, Daniel had been marginalized. However, in these verses, we see Daniel in high office. There are 120 administrators, with three over them, one of whom is Daniel. But because of his exceptional abilities he is set to be prime minister (v. 3).

Daniel's rise to power isn't welcomed by those he has been promoted above. They want him removed. Daniel's personal morality, and his consistent godly living, is recognized by those jealous of him (vv. 4,5). Daniel has modelled the way the New Testament calls us to live (see 1 Pet. 2:11,12).

In verses 6 to 9 we see that the envious administrators come up with a plan that they think will lead to the removal of Daniel from office. They persuade King Darius to pass a law that prohibits anyone from praying to any god. People would only be able to pray to Darius himself. Any contravention to this law means certain death – being thrown in the lions' den.

We can't read chapter 6 without noticing the similarities to chapter 3. In the Aramaic section of the book (chapters 2 – 7) these chapters mirror each other (just as chapter 2 mirrors chapter 7, and chapter 4 mirrors chapter 5). They both open with the king issuing an arrogant law that sets the king up against God. In both chapters, failure to obey the king will lead to certain death (either a fiery furnace or a lions' den). In both chapters, other administrators are opposed to God's people.

These chapters together show us how the world the exiles live in wants the exiles to conform, to be just like it. In chapter 3, we saw the pressure on the exiles to do something God forbade (worship an idol). In chapter 6, we see the pressure on an exile not to do something God commands (pray to Him). Here are the twin pressures God's people always face in the world. They are the sins of commission and omission.

REFLECTION

Where can you find quiet so that you can hear God's voice? What needs to be stripped away from your life to make it ready for Jesus?

DAY 18

READ Daniel 6:10–16

King Darius has issued a decree that allows people to pray, but only to him. It is a law that 'cannot be repealed' (v. 8). Anyone who prays to any other god will be thrown into the lions' den (v. 7).

As in chapter 3, this law threatens the survival of the exiles and therefore the great Old Testament promises of God. If God's people in exile remain faithful to the Lord, and pray to Him, they will be killed in the lions' den.

The pattern of chapter 3 continues to be followed, and again we see the faithfulness of the man of God living in exile. In verse 10 we read of Daniel's response to the decree of the king. We see in this verse that Daniel prays three times each day. His life is absorbed in prayer (not providing a model as to when we should pray, but a good illustration of Ephesians 6:18, where we are called to pray on all occasions). His focus is towards Jerusalem. This is the city that symbolized God living with His people. Now in ruins, Daniel's focus suggests that he believes that God's promises for that city will still be fulfilled. Daniel gives thanks, suggesting he believes that despite the king's order, God is still in control. Further he prays 'just as he had done before'. Godliness when faith is under attack comes more easily when godliness has been shown in times of no attack.

In verses 11 to 16 we see how events unfold. Those jealous of Daniel find him at prayer and report him to the king. The king, bound by his own law, is powerless to do anything and, when reminded again of his law, reluctantly gives the order for Daniel to be thrown to the lions.

We are meant to see the irony in these verses. The chapter opens with the king (as we saw in chapter 3) issuing a law claiming god-like status. And yet by verse 16, we see that Darius has no power to set Daniel free. He even prays that Daniel's God might rescue him. Darius may look the powerful one in control, but he is, in reality, weak and powerless. Indeed, as we note the parallels with chapter 3, here we see a striking difference between Darius's hope and the boastful declaration of Nebuchadnezzar (see 3:15).

That this weak king is not able to do the right thing reminds us of Herod with John the Baptist, and Pilate before the crowd.

REFLECTION

Think of situations where it seems as if those with power in this world look as if they are in control. How does this passage challenge that view?

DAY 19

READ Daniel 6:17–28

Daniel has been thrown into the lions' den. As with the fiery furnace of chapter 3, it looks like the fate of Daniel is inevitable. The description in the narrative of verses 17 and 18 underlines it. Again we see that the powerful king is powerless to help.

In verses 19 and 20 we read of the king going to the lions' den. He speaks about God and Daniel. He declares that God is 'the living God'. The king is using a common OT description of God. He declares that Daniel serves this God continually. His question is whether God has been able to rescue Daniel.

Daniel's reply is that God shut the mouths of the lions. Daniel doesn't explain how He did this. But it is clear that this is (as with the fiery furnace in chapter 3) a miracle from the God who is in complete charge. That this is a miracle is shown in verse 24. Those who have plotted against Daniel now experience what they had planned for him. They are thrown into the lions' den and are overpowered before they reach the floor.

Daniel declares that he is innocent in God's sight. Obedience to the rule of God above the rule of the king has been vindicated as right. Daniel, even though he disobeyed the king's order, has in fact done the right thing, even towards the king (see v. 22). Daniel's clear and faithful stand for God is faith (see Heb. 11:33). It is to live obediently to the Lord, whatever the cost might have been to him.

It is not only those who opposed Daniel who are thrown to the lions. Their families are, too. In our individualistic culture that seems harsh. However, here is a reminder that the actions of an individual ripple beyond that individual, and that God's judgement on the enemies of His people accompanies their rescue.

In verses 25 to 27 we read of Darius's response. Unlike Belshazzar in chapter 5, this response echoes that of Nebuchadnezzar in chapter 4. He also writes a letter to the whole world, testifying to God's rule. Darius's declaration comes at the very centre of the book, and is a good summary of the themes of chapters 1 to 6 (v. 27 reminds us of the God who is in control and saves), and also an introduction to the themes of chapters 7 to 12 (v. 26 tells us of a God who is in control of history, and who will establish an eternal kingdom).

REFLECTION

God has vindicated the faith of Daniel. He did that by rescuing Daniel from the lions' den. Hebrews 11:33 records Daniel as a hero of faith. In which ways is Daniel's faith a model for us?

DAY 20

Review of Daniel 1 – 6

We are now halfway through the book of Daniel. From here on, the style changes and we move away from narrative to 'visions'.

Chapter 1 and 6 both closed by telling us that Daniel lived throughout the whole period of the exile. These six chapters have presented us with a number of themes that it would be important both for these exiles and for later readers to know.

Firstly, we have seen that away from their land and the city of Jerusalem which symbolized God living with His people, God is still both in control and with His people. He has shown that He is the true king, as He has brought Nebuchadnezzar and Darius to praise Him and testify to His rule to the whole world. The Lord is able to humble even the proudest of people opposed to Him. Further, he has shown His rule by bringing judgement on Belshazzar and removing both him and his kingdom.

Secondly, we have seen the witness of faithful servants. In a strange land they have faced the twin pressures to do what God forbids and not do what God commands. We have seen that as they trust God, so they remain faithful to Him under these pressures. God has rescued them not as a promise that He will always rescue His people in this life, but as a demonstration that He is able to rescue, and as a shadow of the true rescue to glory for all who are faithful to Him.

Thirdly, we have seen that the promises of God, to establish an eternal kingdom, will one day be fulfilled. It looks at times in the narrative as if God's promises teeter on the brink of being wiped out. But the God who is King is faithful to the promises He makes.

And fourthly, we see in Daniel a shadow of the Lord Jesus. Innocent, accused, condemned Daniel faces death. But when the stone is rolled away, he is alive. Yet Daniel is a mere shadow of the son of man, who is more clearly revealed in the next chapter.

REFLECTION

Think through the main themes of the book so far. What have been the challenges and encouragements to you as you seek to live faithfully under the rule of Jesus in a world hostile to Him and us?

DAY 21

READ Daniel 7:1–8

The last six chapters of Daniel are less familiar than the first six. However, there is no doubt that we are meant to read on. This chapter is the last part of the section of the book that is written in Aramaic. The rest of the book is written in the Old Testament language of Hebrew. Aramaic was the language of Babylon. Chapters 2 to 7 are therefore a distinct unit within the book. Babylonians can read and understand this section. These chapters have shown us that the Lord is the only God, and that people should humble themselves before Him. The unbeliever in Babylon needs to know this as much as the believer.

Between verses 1 and 2 the narrative changes from the third to the first person. We are reading what Daniel himself wrote down. Verse 1 also dates the chapter. The contents of this chapter take place between chapters 4 and 5. That was the period where Daniel seemed less at the centre of the Babylonian world. He was not, however, forgotten by God. When the world thinks less of us, God does not.

In verse 2, Daniel sees the four winds of heaven churning up the great sea. This is symbolic language that suggests the four compass points by which all wind is described. Later, Jesus will use similar language and speak of four corners of the earth (see Matt. 24:31). Here the whole earth is in view; Daniel is seeing the nations over the whole earth. And from the nations of the world he sees four beasts – beasts that in verse 17 we are told are kingdoms that rise on earth.

The four beasts are increasingly grotesque. You can imagine them as cartoon characters, sketched by an artist. The first is a lion with eagle's wings, but with the feet and heart of a man. Daniel was to see this as Nebuchadnezzar, for Jeremiah had described Nebuchadnezzar as one like a lion and an eagle, and in chapter 4, Nebuchadnezzar actually grew hair like eagle's feathers.

The second beast is a bear with murderous intent. The third beast is a four-winged leopard with four heads. This probably means that it looks for its prey in all directions. And it is given authority to rule. And then comes the fourth beast. We are meant to notice a difference. For Daniel cannot even use any zoological knowledge to describe this beast. It is terrifying. It has ten horns, symbolic of great power. As Daniel ponders the horns, he sees a smaller horn that has eyes and a mouth from which comes boastful words (v. 8).

We will read on and discover the meaning of this vision. But we notice a few things. Firstly, this four-part vision is a parallel to the dream in chapter

2. Then Daniel was being shown that human kingdoms come and go. None last. And readers of Daniel know this has started to happen. The kingdom of Babylon was defeated by the Persians at the end of chapter 5. Secondly, we see all authority on earth is given by God (see v. 6). How comforting to know that our God is bigger than even the most powerful rulers on earth. Thirdly, our God knows the future. It is completely in His control.

REFLECTION

The Lord is revealing the future to Daniel. Spend some time pondering the implications for you that God knows the future of our world and that it is all under His control.

DAY 22

READ Daniel 7:9–12

In verses 11 and 12 Daniel's focus will again be on the smaller horn and the beasts. However, sandwiched between what he sees of them (vv. 2–8 and vv. 11,12) comes a glimpse of glory itself. In verse 9, Daniel looked. The change from prose to poetry catches our attention. It makes this part of the vision stand out.

The reader can't miss the contrasts between what is seen here and what is shown of the beasts. The beasts are hallmarked by aggression and pride. Glory is hallmarked by sovereignty and holiness. The Lord here is called the Ancient of Days. His reign is not limited like the reigns of the beasts. He is eternally God.

The first thing to observe is that Daniel sees God on His throne. You might like to compare what Daniel sees with what the apostle John sees at the start of his vision in Revelation 4. The God of the Bible is always on the throne. It means He is always in complete control of everything that takes place in the universe. How encouraging is this to the exiles (and us) as they live under the tyrannical rule of Belshazzar.

Secondly, we see the holiness of God. His clothing and his hair are white. This is the Bible word for total purity. It means that His rule, again in contrast to the beasts, is good. The language is similar to that used in Revelation 1 to describe the risen and ascended Lord Jesus. Fire symbolizes God's judgement, which is always true and right.

Daniel then sees those who attended the Lord. Presumably angelic beings, here is a picture of both the greatness and majesty of God. It is right that all in heaven acknowledge Him. Again it takes us forward to the angels around the throne that John sees in Revelation 4 and 5.

At the end of verse 10, Daniel sees that this vision is more than just a glimpse of the God of glory. This is a court room, and a trial is about to be heard. Books are opened, as they will be on the Last Day (see Rev. 20:15). When God brings judgement, it will be just. A record has been kept of what everyone has done. And in verses 11 and 12, Daniel sees the judgement come on the beasts. The first is overthrown. For the others, their authority goes, though they continue to exist. Here Daniel is to see that God is totally able to bring His judgement, but is being alerted to a delay before the final judgement.

Here is real encouragement for Daniel. God can, and will, destroy all evil rule. But the fall of Babylon will not mean the end of the world. We, and Daniel, still have to wait for the final overthrow of all evil. But we can be sure that it will happen, and so continue to live as His witnesses in the world.

REFLECTION

How do you think of God? Do you see Him as Lord, King over all, in complete control, only good, and as the judge of all evil? Is our understanding of God too small?

DAY 23

READ Daniel 7:13,14

Now a new character enters the vision that Daniel sees. This is one of the most significant moments in the unfolding of Old Testament revelation. Notice what we are told in verse 13. Firstly, this new character is one 'like a son of man'. Earlier in the vision, Daniel saw a beast 'like a lion' (v. 4). They represent 'kingdoms' that rule (v. 17). At the creation, it was humankind that was to rule the earth. Here Daniel sees a son of man who will one day rule. Here is a glimpse of Eden restored!

Secondly, Daniel sees the son of man coming on the clouds of heaven. Again the contrast is with the beasts. They come out of the sea (v. 3). In Psalm 68:4 it is God who rides on the clouds. The one 'like a son of man' is more than a mere human.

Thirdly, we are told that the son of man was led into the presence of the Ancient of Days. We are meant to be amazed. It suggests that this character has the right to enter into God's presence. Everything we read in the Old Testament to this point has told us that no one can do this. Humanity cannot enter into God's presence. (Look at Isa. 6:1–5, or Ps. 15:1, or Ps. 24:3,4.) But the one like the son of man is led into it!

In verse 14 we are told of the kingdom given to the son of man. Firstly, He is given 'authority, glory and sovereign power'. He is given the right to rule. Like all rule in the book of Daniel, it is given by God (see 2:37). And the rule the Ancient of Days gives here is rule over all humanity – so, 'all peoples, nations and men of every language' all worship Him. Secondly, we are told that the kingdom established by the son of man is eternal. It will neither pass away, nor ever be destroyed. We are meant to see the contrast with the beasts, whose rule only lasts for a time.

Once again (see Dan. 2:44) Daniel is being reassured that the unconditional promises God made to David centuries before will be fulfilled. The universality of the rule of the son of man reminds us that the promises God made to Abraham of blessing to all the world will also be fulfilled. Despite how things seem, all of the great promises of God are on track.

These two verses are of such huge importance that we will come back to them in the next study.

REFLECTION

Can you think of time when it looked as if God was not doing what He has promised? Allow the truth of these verses to encourage you. God's promises are still on track, even at the lowest of times.

DAY 24

READ Mark 14:55–65

In the previous study we saw Daniel's vision of one 'like a son of man'. The same phrase is used of Ezekiel (see Ezek. 36:1). However, in the Gospels the phrase is used by Jesus ninety times to identify Himself! There is no doubt that Jesus saw Himself to be the character of Daniel's vision.

In Luke 17, Jesus sees the kingdom of God and the days of the Son of Man being fulfilled at His return (see Luke 17:22–37). In the section of Luke where it comes (17:11 – 19:27), Jesus is concerned that people understand how to be ready for that day, how to have a place in the eternal kingdom; He asks, '...when the Son of Man comes, will he find faith on the earth?' (Luke 18:8).

In the passage we have read, Jesus is on trial before the Sanhedrin. In verse 61 they directly ask Him whether He is the Christ. Notice the echoes of Daniel 7 in Jesus' reply. Jesus is saying, as He had to the disciples in Mark 8:38, that the day of the Son of Man is a day of inescapable judgement. Stephen, when put to death, sees the Son of Man standing at the right hand of God (Acts 7:56). Jesus is already in the position of all authority. We await His return as Son of Man, to bring salvation for those who are ready, and judgement for those who have rejected Him.

In the last book of the Bible, John is given a 'revelation' of the future, of 'what must soon take place' (Rev. 1:1). He is told to write to the seven churches of Asia. He turns to see who is commanding him. The one speaking to, and standing among, the churches is one 'like a son of man'. Again the echoes of Daniel 7 are clear. As John sees the future, and as he sees the judgement on the world in the sixth seal (see Rev. 6), so he also sees people from every nation, tribe and tongue standing before the Lamb, singing in praise (Rev. 7:9,10).

It means we can be even more certain than Daniel that the promised kingdom will come, because the Son of Man has already been born, has died and has been raised to God's right hand. We wait eagerly for the days of the Son of Man.

REFLECTION

Is this how you think of Jesus? Ponder what impact this vision of Jesus ought to have on our lives. Further, given that every knee will bow before Jesus (see Phil. 2:10), what does this mean for our personal evangelism?

DAY 25

READ Daniel 7:15–18

The content of the revelation given to Daniel has come to an end. Twice we are told in verse 15 of Daniel's response to them. He is 'troubled in spirit'; the visions 'disturbed' him. It is reminiscent of the reaction that Nebuchadnezzar had back in chapter 2 – his 'mind was troubled and he could not sleep'. In both cases, Gentile Nebuchadnezzar and Jewish Daniel needed interpretation of the visions that they had seen.

In both cases, the interpretation of what was seen comes from 'outside' the one who has had the vision. In chapter 2, Daniel prayed to the God of heaven 'concerning the mystery' (2:18) and it was 'revealed to Daniel' (2:19). Here Daniel asks 'one of those standing there' (v. 16). In later chapters, we will see angels explain Daniel's visions. Here the one 'standing there' gave Daniel 'the interpretation of these things' (v. 16b). In other words, what follows are not Daniel's own thoughts, but the authoritative word from God. It is a good reminder to us to take seriously what we are about to read.

Verses 16b to 18 are the summary of the meaning of the dream. First, we are told about the four beasts. They represent 'four kingdoms that will rise from the earth'. They mirror the dream Nebuchadnezzar had of the four-part gold statue in chapter 2. The same idea is being repeated here. Human kingdoms come and go!

However, there is now a contrast with what happened in chapter 2. In that chapter, the focus was on God setting up a kingdom that will never be destroyed. God is here described as 'the Most High', rather than the 'Ancient of Days'. A very common description of God in Daniel, it emphasizes His rule over that of anything else.

In the summary in verse 18, the emphasis is on the saints. Saints in the Bible doesn't mean an elite subset of believers, but all believers. And so it is all believers who will receive the kingdom. And with repeated emphasis, Daniel is told they will 'possess it for ever – yes, for ever and ever' (v. 18). Here are the exiles being assured that not only will the great promises of a kingdom be fulfilled, but also that God's people will enjoy that kingdom for ever. Daniel may live now in the kingdom of the Babylonians, but one day he will possess this eternal kingdom. History is heading towards a final goal.

REFLECTION

Like Daniel we live in this world, but are also destined for God's eternal kingdom. We are even now 'citizens of heaven' (see Phil. 3:20), and are 'seated...in the heavenly realms' (Eph. 2:6). How amazing is it to have our eternal destiny assured?

DAY 26

READ Daniel 7:19–22

In the last few verses, the angel has been explaining the meaning of the four beasts that Daniel saw. But Daniel wants to know more. And in particular he wants to know the meaning of the fourth beast. This is the beast that was 'different from all the others'. The differences are spelled out. This fourth beast is the 'most terrifying' as it 'crushed and devoured its victims and trampled underfoot whatever was left' (v. 19).

Daniel is also concerned to understand some of the details of what he has seen earlier. In particular he wants to know about the horns. He wants to understand the ten horns on the fourth beast, but also about the little horn – the horn that 'looked more imposing than the others' and 'spoke boastfully.'(v. 20)

However, before the interpretation comes, as Daniel is asking his questions, he now sees more in the vision (vv. 21,22). The boastful horn is at war against God's people, the saints. Here Daniel is seeing that God's people are opposed.

This is important preparation for Daniel and the people who read this after their return from exile in Babylon. Daniel is being shown the future. After they return from exile, there will still be opposition (described as 'war') against the saints. Here is a theme that will be explained further in the later chapters. When God's people return from exile (which they will do within decades of Daniel having this dream), it will not be the establishment of the final, eternal kingdom. Instead, God's people are to expect further future opposition. And, in verse 21, they will be defeated by this dreadful 'horn'.

However, the assurance comes in verse 22. This opposition will not last forever. The opposition to the people of God is limited. The reason is spelled out. The Ancient of Days will come and pronounce judgement in favour of the saints. Believers are on the winning side!

But this is not because they can overthrow this boastful horn. Deliverance and victory will come to them only because the Ancient of Days is on their side. And that is when the saints will possess the kingdom. In the next verses, the explanation of the dream will be given.

REFLECTION

Be humbled and reassured by these verses; humbled by the truth that saints are not strong enough by themselves to defeat those who oppose them, but encouraged that the Ancient of Days is. There is coming a time when He will deliver us to the kingdom. Look forward to that day!

DAY 27

READ Daniel 7:23–28

We now come to the explanation of the dream. There are lots of parallels with the dream Nebuchadnezzar had in chapter 2. Once again there is mention of four kingdoms. But now the emphasis is on the universal devastation that the fourth kingdom will bring (v. 23). We then come to the ten horns. The horn is a Bible metaphor for strength. They seem to come from the fourth beast. They represent ten kings who simultaneously rule on the earth.

In verse 24 the focus is on another king. Then follows a description of his rule. He is blasphemous against God; he oppresses God's people. He tries to overturn the laws of nature. God's people will be ruled by him for a limited time (v. 25).

Commentators spend much time trying to identify who these characters are. The four beasts are most likely the successive empires of Babylon, Persia, Greece and Rome. But beyond that, things are harder to work out. Indeed, it is not altogether clear whether the references to 'after them' (v. 24) are meant to be read chronologically. Many translations have these verses as poetry, suggesting we don't read them literally. Some identify the king of verse 24 as Antiochus Epiphanes IV, king of Seleucia, who destroyed the Temple in Jerusalem in 167 BC.

The main point, though, is once again the 'but' at the start of verse 26. Just as in verses 18 and 22, here is the language of contrast. Kings will come and go. Evil rulers, opposed to God, His people and His natural order will arise and oppress the people of God. But! In verse 26 the court of judgement sits and his power is taken away and he is destroyed forever.

Instead, one day, the wicked rule of humankind will be replaced. One day, God's people, the saints, will be given rule (v. 27). In the last book of the Bible, John sees God's people reigning with Christ for ever (Rev. 22:5). Once again we are to look forward to all of God's promises being fulfilled.

In verse 28 we read of Daniel's response to the vision and its explanation. What he has seen troubles him and he decides to keep the matter to himself. At least until he writes it down. What Daniel has begun to see is that the immediate future for God's people contains oppression and suffering. God's people, however, can cling to the assurance that the eternal promises of God will one day be fulfilled.

We have come to the end of the part of the book that is written in the Babylonian language of Aramaic, so Babylonians could learn the lessons of these chapters as well as the Jews. The overall message is that Daniel's God is the one in ultimate control. Living under His rule is the only eternally secure way to live.

REFLECTION

Although the eternal future for God's people is utterly secure, until that day God's people live in a world where evil often rules and God's people are opposed. It has always been like this for the people of God – we should be realists about the world we live in.

DAY 28

READ Daniel 8:1–8

We now enter the last section of the book. But there are clear connections with what has come before. We are reading again of a vision Daniel has seen. The line in verse 1 'after the one that had already appeared to me' means we are meant to read this chapter alongside chapter 7. Further, the date of this vision, 'In the third year of King Belshazzar's reign', means it has come only two years after the vision in chapter 7. The pattern of the chapter is also familiar. We are first allowed to read the content of the dream. It is then followed by the interpretation, rather like the dreams of Nebuchadnezzar in chapters 2 and 4, or Daniel in chapter 7.

A quick glance at the chapter, however, shows some differences with what has come before. Firstly, the location of the vision. In chapter 7 it is 'the great sea' (7:2). Here we are in Susa, beside the Ulai Canal. It seems we are closer to the action; moving from the broader horizon to a more concrete situation. Secondly, the description of the animals. In chapter 7 the beasts were composite beasts, like cartoon characters. Here we are dealing with recognizable farm animals. Thirdly, within the dream and its interpretation comes angelic commentary (e.g. in vv. 13,14).

In verses 3 to 4 our focus is on the ram. The difference between the two horns suggests the growth of an empire. This is an empire at war. It conquers west, north and south, and is without rival in the world: 'He did as he pleased and became great' (v.4).

As Daniel is pondering what he saw, a second animal is introduced. At the height of the great power of the ram comes a goat with a single horn. The goat comes with great speed; his feet don't even touch the ground (v. 5b). The arrival of the goat brings about a total reversal. In verse 4, no animal could stand against the ram. But in verse 7, the ram is powerless to stand against the goat. In verse 4, none could be rescued from the ram's power. But in verse 7, none could rescue the ram from the goat's power. What seemed spectacular about the ram is now superseded by the goat. The ram 'did as he pleased and became great' but the goat became very great (v. 8). Verse 8 concludes, however, with the indication that this powerful goat will not last. Its single horn is replaced by four powerful horns.

Before we allow ourselves to look at the interpretation of the dream, we can easily deduce a number of points. Firstly, as the book of Daniel has repeatedly shown us, human kingdoms come and go. No human rule lasts for ever. No single ruler, or human empire, has lasted. Secondly, humans grab rule, usually through fighting and war. Humankind was created in the image of God to rule. But sin means that instead of being given rule by God and governing for the benefit of others, we take rule for ourselves and seek to do as we please.

REFLECTION

What we have read in this chapter so far describes things on an international scale. But the sin of humankind is not just seen in the macro. Ponder how we see similar patterns to chapter 8 in our own communities and families.

So far, in this vision, we have read of the ram and the goat. The power of the ram was replaced by the goat in verses 5 to 8. But at the end of verse 8 the power of the goat was being replaced, too. Its power, represented by its horn, was replaced by four prominent horns. It is out of one of them that another horn comes.

As we read verses 9 to 14 we are meant to spot some differences to the descriptions of verses 1 to 8. In verses 9 to 14 the descriptions of the horn become more impressionistic. Further, the language of war now takes on a hostility towards God as well as other nations.

In verse 9 the horn grows in power towards 'the Beautiful Land'. The phrase has been used by Ezekiel (20:6,15) where it is clearly Israel. But the attack from this 'horn' is more than just a physical conflict. In verse 10 we are told that it grew until 'it reached the host of the heavens'. Taken with what we will read in chapter 10, it indicates that there is a supernatural aspect to the conflict. A more sinister power is at work than merely a human ruler.

In verse 11 this ruler sets himself up 'to be as great as the Prince of the host'. His attack is against God Himself. And, as is usual in the Bible, an attack against God is seen in an attack on His people. So this horn will take away the daily sacrifice of God's people and the 'place of [God's] sanctuary was brought low'. This horn will attack at the heart of Israel, the Temple in Jerusalem.

This attack is described in verse 12 as 'rebellion'. This horn is in rebellion against God, and so attacks the host (or saints) and sets itself up as the object of worship. It prospers, appearing all-powerful, even seeming to throw truth to the ground. This attack is as bad as the exile attack by Nebuchadnezzar.

What is happening is awful. And it leads one of the holy ones, probably angels, to ask, 'How long will it take for the vision to be fulfilled...?' (v. 13). The cry echoes the psalmist (see Ps. 74:10 as one example), wondering for how long the Lord will allow such rebellion against Him and His people. The question is answered in verse 14: 'It will take 2,300 evenings and mornings'.

What can we deduce from what Daniel sees? When we come to the interpretation, the exact identity of this horn is not given (unlike the goat, v. 21). We can guess at a first fulfilment in the awful attack on Jerusalem by Antiochus Epiphanes IV in 167 BC. He attacked Jerusalem, forbade Jewish worship, and built a pagan altar in the Temple. But the lack of specific identification and the time period mentioned (close to three and a half years) suggests we should read this with a wider horizon. In Revelation 12, John sees God's people attacked by the dragon, or devil, for the same period. We are probably meant to understand that God will always be rebelled against, and therefore God's people will also always be opposed. However notice the time is limited (v. 14). There will be an end to this. The martyrs in heaven utter the same cry (Rev. 6:10). They too are similarly reassured.

REFLECTION

All around us we see people living in rebellion against God. All Christians know something of that in their experience of rejection and opposition. Ponder the realism of this vision, and yet also the hope. It will come to an end!

DAY 30

READ Daniel 8:15–27

By himself, Daniel is unable to interpret the vision he has seen. Whoever the one 'like a man' is in verse 15, it is clear that Daniel will need heavenly help to understand the vision. And so the angel Gabriel is told to give Daniel its meaning (v. 16).

Gabriel first tells Daniel that the vision concerns 'the time of the end' (v. 17). Given what follows, it is unlikely that we are meant to think 'the end of all things', but rather the end of someone's rebellion against God, as He brings judgement on them. Just as the exile had been an 'end' of Judah's rebellion, so there will be an 'end' to the future evil Daniel is allowed to see (see v. 25b).

Daniel is given the interpretation of the dream in verses 20 to 25. The ram of verse 3 is identified as the kings of Media and Persia. The goat is the king of Greece, with the horn being Alexander the Great. The Greek empire would be divided into four parts (v. 22). It is, however only one part that Daniel needs to know about (v. 23). The stern-faced king refers to Antiochus. The word 'stern-faced' is used (in Hebrew) of the adulterous woman in Proverbs 7:13. She is the opposite of wisdom. Here Antiochus is also the master of intrigue. Daniel is being given a portrait of this future ruler. He will be very strong, will be against God's people (v. 24), and so be opposed to God Himself (v. 25).

Daniel must understand that the return from exile which he will witness is not going to be the time when God's promises to Abraham and David will be fulfilled. Before that there will be times of real suffering, as tyrants like Antiochus will arise and will oppose God's people. However, Daniel is to be reassured – 'he will be destroyed', but it will not be 'by human power' (v. 25b). God is still in control and He will overthrow such rulers. The New Testament tells us that Antiochus is only one in a line of those who will oppose God's people. Like Daniel, we can be encouraged that their downfall is certain.

The conclusion of the chapter tells us what Daniel is to do. In verse 26, what he has seen is 'true' and he is to 'seal up the vision, for it concerns the distant future'. It probably means that Daniel is not being given prophecy about the immediate times that he needs to proclaim. Some of what he has seen will only be fulfilled four centuries later. Although Daniel is 'appalled by the vision' (v. 27), later readers will see that God has all history under control. And every 'antichrist' will be destroyed.

REFLECTION

Notice Daniel's response to the vision in verse 27. He 'got up and went about the king's business'. Knowing God was in control of the future meant he could continue to his normal life in the present. What impact should God's sovereign control make on you?

DAY 31

READ Daniel 9:1–3

These verses are the foundation of the prayer that will follow from verse 4. First we are told the date of the prayer – 'the first year of Darius son of Xerxes'. It is very probable that Darius is another name for Cyrus, mentioned back in chapter 1 (see 1:21). This will help us see (e.g. Ezra 1:1) that the prayer of Daniel is answered. Darius being 'made ruler' over the Babylonian empire is something God has done. Again we see He is in control, even of pagan kings.

In verse 2 we see that Daniel is aware of the prophecies of Jeremiah. There are two phrases Daniel uses to describe what Jeremiah has spoken. Firstly, they are Scripture, and secondly they are the 'word of the LORD'. These are terms Jesus uses to describe the Old Testament. It means that Daniel, within decades of Jeremiah speaking, accepts that the prophet's words carry the authority of any other part of the Old Testament.

Daniel knew that Jeremiah had prophesied that the 'desolation of Jerusalem would last seventy years' (v. 2). He had prophesied that the exile would happen but the 'whole country will become a desolate wasteland, and these nations will serve the king of Babylon for seventy years' (Jer. 25:11). Further, he had written a letter to the elders in exile saying, '"...you will call upon me and... find me when you seek me with all your heart. I will be found by you,"' declares the LORD, 'and will bring you back from captivity' (Jer. 29:12–14).

Daniel's prayer is, therefore, founded on Scripture. Verse 3 follows verse 2 with a 'so'. It indicates that Daniel is responding to the word of God. He is now 'calling upon the Lord' as Jeremiah said should happen. Daniel, therefore, believes the word of God, expecting Him to do what He had said. Praying according to the promises of God is a sound basis for our praying, too. In order to do this we have to know the 'word of the LORD'.

We notice, too, the serious nature of the praying. In verse 3 we are told that Daniel 'pleaded' with the Lord. He also fasts, something often associated in the Old Testament with prayer. And he wears sackcloth and ashes, which are Old Testament expressions of mourning. Daniel is not just going to ask God to honour His promises, but is going to confess the sins that have led to the exile judgement of God.

REFLECTION

How well do we know what God has promised for us? Are we in the habit of using the promises of God as the foundation for our praying? Is there the same seriousness in our praying as we see here in Daniel?

DAY 32

READ Daniel 9:4–19

Daniel now prays to the covenant God. He acknowledges the rightness of the Lord's prior judgement on Judah. God has been right to bring the exile. In verses 4 to 6, Daniel has got his thesaurus out – 'sinned, done wrong, wicked, rebelled'. But he explains how this happened. By '[turning] away from your commands and laws' and then not listening to His prophets. Judah had rejected the word of God. This is not new theology here from Daniel. What he is confessing is what we have all done since the Garden of Eden. Rejecting the word of God is sin.

In verse 7 we see the right judgement of God on sin. He 'scattered' the people. Just as God had scattered humankind in the judgement of Babel, so He has done in judgement on Judah's (and Israel's) unfaithfulness. In both verses 7 and 8 Daniel calls this judgement 'shame'. And in verses 8 to 11a he spells out repeatedly the rightness of God to bring this about. However, Daniel also knows that the Lord is merciful and forgiving.

In verses 11b to 14 Daniel acknowledges three times that the people had been warned that exile would be the judgement for disobedience. Leviticus 26 and Deuteronomy 28 had been crystal clear – '...if you will not listen to me and carry out all these commands... then I will do this to you' (Lev 26:14–16). Having issued the warning, God would not have been righteous if He hadn't carried it out.

In verses 15 to 19 we hear Daniel's petition. As he continues to acknowledge the people's sin, he now pleads for the Lord to 'turn away your anger and your wrath from Jerusalem' (v. 16), to 'look with favour on your desolate sanctuary' (v. 17), and to 'forgive' (v. 19). However, the focus of his prayer is centred on the Lord's 'name'. He begins his petition by remembering that the rescue from Egypt centuries earlier 'made for yourself a name'. The Lord's name is a reflection of who He truly is. Jerusalem and the people bear the Lord's name. And so Daniel prays that the Lord would act 'for [His] sake'.

In the New Testament, Jesus teaches that our prayers should first focus on God's name, His reputation. 'Father, hallowed be your name' (Luke 11:2) Further, the apostle Paul tells us that God's rescue of us through the gospel is also 'for his name's sake' (Rom. 1:5).

REFLECTION

Do we acknowledge our sinfulness in our prayers? Do we acknowledge that judgement is what we rightly deserve from the Lord? How far is our praying motivated by a deep concern for the name and reputation of the Lord?

DAY 33

READ Daniel 9:20–27

In verses 20 to 21 Daniel is interrupted in his praying. The angel Gabriel, who Daniel had seen during the vision in chapter 8, once again appears to him. In verses 22 to 23 Gabriel explains that he has come to give him insight and understanding. Daniel's prayer has been answered! The Lord has heard his prayer and has responded. He is now to give thought to the message and understand the vision, which is described in verses 24 to 27.

Verse 24 speaks of 'seventy "sevens"' decreed for God's people. The numbers are likely to be symbolic. Seventy is the perfect long period of time. Seven is the number of completeness. It therefore refers to a 'perfect or completed time'. It is the period required for the six things mentioned in verse 24 to be completed. The return from exile will signal the end of the judgement on Judah's sin, and the positive establishment of a new temple. By listing six things here it is as if the exile ending is like a new creation. Daniel knows enough from chapters 7 and 8 to know that their return isn't finally Eden restored. But it is a shadow of the end time. The seventy 'sevens' could, therefore, refer to the rest of time, from the return from exile to the return of Jesus.

In verse 25 there is more information of the seventy sevens. These will be broken into seven sevens and sixty-two sevens. At the start will be the restoration of Jerusalem, which is not going to be easy (v. 25). Then after sixty-two sevens, an 'Anointed One' will be cut off. There is much debate as to whether this is referring to Cyrus at the return from exile (who gave the order for the Temple in Jerusalem to be rebuilt, and is called 'anointed' in Isa. 45:1), or to events in the second century BC. However, it is almost certainly also looking forward to the comings of Jesus.

It is certainly Jesus who confirms the covenant (v. 27). Jesus speaks also of an 'abomination that causes desolation' as still to happen (Mark 13:14). And so it could be that the final 'seven' refers to the period between the two comings of Jesus. The events of verse 27 could then refer to the destruction of the Temple in AD 70. What is clear is that the world will get no better. Wars will continue to the end (as Jesus also said, Mark 13:8). But those set against God will be dealt with (v. 27b).

REFLECTION

We are living in the last 'seven' of human history. We are living in the last days (Acts 2:17). What impact does that have on you as you live in a world opposed to God and His people?

DAY 34

READ Daniel 10:1–9

These verses begin the final section of the book. Chapters 10 to 12 are all one long section that describe Daniel's final dream. Verse 1 tells us the date; the third year of the reign of Cyrus. Chapter 1 told us that he remained in high office in the land until the first year of King Cyrus. That was the year the exile ended. Seventy years later, he would be well into his eighties. In the third year of Cyrus, two years after more than forty thousand people returned from exile to Jerusalem, here is Daniel, still in Babylon receiving his final vision.

The vision concerns 'a great war'. Daniel takes it very seriously (v. 2). He mourns for three weeks and eats 'no choice food'. It is similar to the action taken by Daniel in chapter 1. By the end of the dream Daniel will be able to 'go on his way' (see 12:13), but here there is mourning at the thought of war.

Daniel is standing by the great river Tigris, the river that today runs through the centre of Baghdad. He looks up and sees, in verses 5 to 6, 'a man dressed in linen, with a belt of the finest gold round his waist. His body was like chrysolite, his face like lightning, his eyes like flaming torches, his arms and legs like the gleam of burnished bronze, and his voice like the sound of a multitude.' We have no trouble identifying this man. In John's vision of one 'like a son of man', the details are very similar to what Daniel sees (look up Rev. 1:12–16) This is the one Daniel saw in chapter 7 approach the Ancient of Days to be given all rule and authority. This is a pre-incarnate vision of Jesus.

Those with Daniel don't see what he sees (v. 7). Instead they flee, leaving Daniel alone without strength, afraid and helpless (v. 8). As he listens, he falls into a deep sleep. John's response when he sees the vision of the ascended Christ is similar. At one level this is the right response to Jesus, King of heaven. We ought to be struck with awe.

Daniel is being shown who lies behind the unfolding of human history that the vision will focus on. It will give him confidence that what he is going to see is true. He needn't, therefore, be afraid of what he sees. It is under the hand of the one 'like a son of man'.

REFLECTION

Jesus is the one who stands behind both the Scriptures and the future it tells us about. Are you in awe of this Jesus? And have you got confidence that what He reveals is true? We needn't be afraid of the future!

DAY 35

READ Daniel 10:10 – 11:1

In verses 1 to 9 Daniel has seen the one who stands behind the vision he is about to see. But before the vision comes, Daniel is 'touched' and spoken to. In verse 10 a hand touched the trembling Daniel. This hand is an angel. Daniel is told to consider the words he is about to hear. Here is how heaven thinks we should treat the Word of God. Consider carefully!

In verse 12 the heavenly voice tells Daniel that his prayers have been heard. The speaker has come in response to them. But in verse 13 he says that he has been delayed by the prince of Persia and that he needed the angelic help of Michael. The ideas might seem strange, but we are being introduced to the fact that there are heavenly realities beyond our world. Behind the rulers on earth stand angelic princes. Earthly conflicts are but echoes of battles in heavenly realms. The New Testament speaks of such conflict, too (e.g. Eph. 6:12). Daniel is, however, now going to be told what will happen to the Jews in the future. Here is a reminder that God hears His people when they pray, but that there can be delays in His answers.

In verses 15 to 17 we hear Daniel's response. At first he is speechless, but for a second time he is 'touched', now on his lips, and he is able to speak. The vision makes him feel helpless, unworthy and without strength. Understanding reality beyond this world has left Daniel awestruck.

Once again, verse 18, Daniel is touched by the one who is speaking with him. He is told to be at peace, and to be strong. Daniel acknowledges in verse 19 that the touch and the words have indeed brought him strength and he is now ready to see the vision and hear God's word to him. For Daniel to receive the word of God requires God to be at work in him. The same is true with us. We need God's gracious 'touch' in order to properly hear His word.

In 10:20 to 11:1 Daniel is told he is about to be hear what is written in the Book of Truth. What will happen in the future is so under the control of God that He already has it written down! After revealing this truth to Daniel, the angel can return to his heavenly work (v. 20). Once again, Daniel is being told that behind human, political and international affairs is the work of angels in heaven.

REFLECTION

Daniel knows he needs strength from God to hear and accept God's word. Are we in the habit of humbly coming before the Lord and asking for His strength as we read the Bible? Are we awestruck that God has already got the future written down?

DAY 36

READ Daniel 11:2–20

Daniel is now ready to see the vision, to hear what is written in the Book of Truth. Verses 2 to 4 are describing the move of power from Persia as the dominant ruler, to Greece. It is a replay of what was explicitly told us back in chapter 8. There will be three further kings in Persia, then a mighty king will come. This is almost certainly fulfilled in Alexander the Great. But in verse 4 the kingdom will be uprooted and given to others. Daniel is being told what will happen. But it is worth noting the verb at the end of verse 4. Alexander's empire will not be 'taken' by others but be 'given' to them. This is a repeated theme in the book of Daniel. Human rule is given by God.

Verses 5 to 20 tell what will happen after that. Daniel is told about a king of the south and a king of the north. Who are they? It is likely that they are kings north and south of the Beautiful Land. The place mentioned in verse 16 is almost certainly a title for Judah, God's land. To the north lies Syria, and to the south lies Egypt. Daniel is being told of the battles that will come between the kings of Syria and Egypt, and the power struggles between the two. Here is a description of the periods after Alexander the Great right up to the time of Seleucus IV, king of Syria.

The conflict between these two kingdoms will impact Judah, who lies between the two. In verse 14, 'violent men among your own people' will rebel against the south but without success. The king of the north becomes stronger and Egypt becomes powerless (v. 15). The invader can do as he wishes, and the Beautiful Land is invaded (v. 16), as it was at the beginning of Daniel. Judah is destroyed. Antiochus III makes a marriage alliance with Egypt again in verse 17. He seems totally on the rampage in verse 18. However, even he will be destroyed (v. 19). He is succeeded by a king we know was Seleucid IV (v. 20).

We read these verses a long time after the events described here have happened. It means we can read secular history books and see how meticulously Daniel is being told about international events over the next three centuries. He is even told of the temporary alliances that are formed between nations through marriage (e.g. in v. 6 and v. 17).

What this means for Daniel (and his first readers) is that when the return from exile happened, it would not be the time when all God's promises would be fulfilled. God's people would have to be patient. However, they are being told that God is totally in control; He knows the future! And further, there are still going to be difficult times ahead for them.

REFLECTION

How amazing is it that God not only knows the future big picture, but that He knows every detail of it. Even down to the marriage alliances among nations! We serve a very big and powerful God: one we can trust is in total control of His world.

DAY 37

READ Daniel 11:21–35

We continue to read of the vision given to Daniel. However, from verse 21 the pace slows and our attention is focused on the successor to Seleucid IV. He was Seleucid's brother, rather than direct royal descent, and his rise to power is unexplained. Although from the start we know his reign will not be long, a large amount of space is given to this man, Antiochus Epiphanes. We came across him in 8:23.

Verses 21 to 28 describe his hunger for power. He sweeps away huge armies, and also the 'prince of the covenant', most likely a pro-Egyptian high priest in Judah (v. 22). He wants to invade Egypt. Powerful armies stand against each other (vv. 25,26). Verse 27 hints at an attempt by the king of Egypt at diplomacy - they sit at the same table. Neither party can be trusted, and Antiochus will leave to return home.

In verse 28, on his return, Antiochus travels through Israel, and his heart is set against God's people. In verse 29 Antiochus tries to invade Egypt, but he is unable to. Ships from the western coastlands will oppose him. This is a probably a reference to the emerging Roman Empire.

This setback will make Antiochus furious. We have been told, in verse 21, he is 'a contemptible person', proud and arrogant. When he loses, he lashes out at God's people (v. 30). Some will forsake the covenant. Antiochus's forces will come to Jerusalem (v. 31). He will stop the daily sacrifices there. And he will set up the abomination that causes desolation. Historians tell us that Antiochus put an altar to the Greek god Zeus on the place where the burnt offering was made. And there he offered pigs as a sacrifice.

Verse 32 tells us that there are two responses that Jews will make. Some will be corrupted by flattery, but others will remain faithful and resist Antiochus. Those who know God, called the 'wise' (v. 33), stand firmly, but some will die by the sword. Under the persecution Antiochus brings, as he totally destroys the second temple built in Jerusalem, some 'will stumble' (v. 35), which probably means they will die. They won't be saved from death by a miracle, like Daniel and his friends were. But it will be for a purpose. Their death will be the means by which they are 'refined, purified and made spotless'. For God's true people death is not the end, but merely the final means of God making us like Jesus.

One idea runs through these verses. God's people are being told awful trouble will come 'but only for a time' (v. 24); things will happen at the 'appointed time' (vv. 27,35). God's people will later read these verses and be encouraged. God allows men like

Antiochus to do dreadful things; it is still under His control. Jesus uses the language that describes what Antiochus will do (setting up an 'abomination that causes desolation') and says it will happen again (Matt. 24:15). Antiochus wasn't the first and won't be the last to contemptibly set himself against God's people. But ultimately they don't last for ever.

REFLECTION

Ponder how the world seeks to tempt us to be 'flattered' and to 'violate the covenant'. The only way to 'resist' is to know their God (v. 32). How can we do that more and more?

DAY 38

READ Daniel 11:36–45

So far in chapter 11 Daniel has seen events that would take place over the next three centuries, right up to the rule of Antiochus Epiphanes. However, at verse 36 the focus changes. A king is now in view. But it is unlikely that we are now reading about Antiochus. He didn't do as he pleased. And the battles described don't fit with any known ancient history. So we are now looking beyond his time. A king will come who thinks himself a god, and will speak against the true God. His god appears to be military, as he attacks others. He gives his honour to idolatry and to those who will acknowledge him (v. 39).

Verse 40 gives us a clue that we are looking towards the end of time. There will be war. In verse 41 we see that this king will invade the Beautiful Land. He will oppose God's people. His influence will be international (v. 42). He will control financial institutions (v. 43). Again in verse 45 we see that he is set against God and His people, as he sets his tents at the beautiful holy mountain. This is language that reminds us of the place where God made a covenant with His people. But the key is verse 45b: '… he will come to his end, and no one will help him.'

Every reader has wondered who this king is. Daniel's description of him uses the familiar language of the vision. He uses the names of the nations of the time and speaks of God's people in Old Testament terms. We are, however, probably meant to see this character as a future personification of evil. It is very likely that the person outlined in Daniel 11 is the same as that described by Paul in 2 Thessalonians 2. In verse 4 of that chapter, Paul writes, 'He will oppose and will exalt himself over everything that is called God or is worshipped, so that he sets himself up in God's temple, proclaiming himself to be God.'

The language is very similar to that in Daniel's vision. Paul calls him 'the man of lawlessness'. He hadn't come when Paul was writing. Paul sees this man coming soon before the day of the Lord Jesus' return. Paul assures his readers that while his power is at work in the world now, when he arrives in this world, Jesus will sweep him away with the mere breath of His mouth.

Many generations have wondered whether some evil ruler in their day was this man of lawlessness. What we can be sure of, though, is that he won't finally win. He is no match for the true and eternal King.

REFLECTION

Paul's application of the teaching about the man of lawlessness is to 'stand firm and hold to the teachings we passed on to you' (2 Thess. 2:15).What does it mean to stand firm? And how, in practice, do we hold to apostolic teaching?

DAY 39

READ Daniel 12:1–4

Daniel is told that close to the end there will be a time of unparalleled distress. It fits with what we read in 2 Thessalonians and Revelation 20. During that time, God's people are protected by Michael. During the distress there is heavenly help for the people of God. The distress signals the very end. There is, however, that 'but' in the middle of verse 1! God's people will be delivered. The people are those whose names are written 'in the book'. This is the Lamb's book of life mentioned in Revelation 20:11–15. It contains the names of all the people who will be delivered.

In verse 2, Daniel speaks of resurrection. Everyone who has died ('who sleep in the dust' picks up the language of Gen. 3:19, 'to dust you will return') will awake, and will be raised. No one will miss this day. But it will be a day of division. For some, those with names in the book, this is resurrection to life. But for others it is everlasting contempt. This means being eternally shamed, day after day, for all eternity. This division, and these two eternal destinations, are expanded greatly by Jesus in the Gospels. He speaks of the division in parables like the wise and foolish virgins, or the sheep and goats (see Matt. 25). Everlasting contempt is a place of darkness, weeping and gnashing of teeth.

In verse 3 we are given a description of what everlasting life will be like. Those there will 'shine like the brightness of the heavens', shining 'like the stars for ever and ever'. This is impressionistic language. It carries the idea of not merely surviving, but of being part of the heavenly court, being glorified. It is something that will be brilliant. Those who will receive this are called 'wise' and those 'who lead many to righteousness'. Being wise in the Old Testament means to fear God and shun evil. It is to be a person who repents and believes the gospel. Leading people to righteousness is a reminder that being believers means being involved in enabling others to do the same.

Verse 4 tells us we are near the end of the book. It is to be sealed, or kept safe, and will be read until the end of time. People may search everywhere for knowledge. But the knowledge God's people need is to be found here in the Scriptures.

REFLECTION

How brilliant it is to know our future – to know that after death believers will one day rise and enjoy glory for ever. We need the eternal perspective that we find in Daniel, so that we will continue to be wise and lead others to righteousness.

DAY 40

READ Daniel 12:5–13

Having seen a glimpse of the end in verses 1 to 4, it is no surprise that one of those with Daniel asks the question, 'How long will it be before these astonishing things are fulfilled?' (v. 6). People have always been asking questions about when the end of the world will come!

The answer comes in verse 7, 'It will be for a time, times and half of time.' We had that phrase in chapter 7. It was the rule of the fourth beast. It is three and a half years, or forty-two months. The same period of time is mention in the book of Revelation (Rev. 12:14). It indicates that time is fixed and that time in this world is far from perfect (it is half of seven, which represents perfection). Time will continue until the power of, or over, the holy people (that is, God's people), will be completed.

In response to this, Daniel asks, 'what will the outcome of all this be?' (v. 8). Daniel is told to 'go your way' (see vv. 9,13). That is the application of the vision that he has seen. He is just to keep going, living as God's person in this world. He is to keep going until the end comes. Until it does, things will carry on as before. Many will be 'refined', while the wicked will continue to be wicked.

In verses 11 to 12 we again get time references. Scholars debate the number of days; 1,290 is close to the three and a half years mentioned. It is another reference to the period of time in which we live. But then blessing is promised for the person who reaches the end of the 1,335 days! If we remember that numbers in the book of Daniel are symbolic rather than literal, it is possible that objectively the time is symbolically fixed at 1,290 days (although scholars debate this issue). However, because this age is an age of persecution and suffering, it will feel more like 1,335 days. The hardships of this world make the wait for the coming kingdom seem longer that it really is.

REFLECTION

Think back through the whole of the book of Daniel. Ponder some of the big themes that we have seen. Remember how Daniel was called to live while in exile, while waiting for God's promises to be fulfilled. What impact will the book of Daniel have on your life?

REFERENCES

[1] *Surprised by Joy* (London: HarperCollins, 2002).

MORE IN THIS SERIES

ROMANS: Momentous News *By David Cook*

ISBN: 978-1-906173-24-1

MARK: The Suffering Servant *By Jeremy McQuoid*

ISBN: 978-1-906173-55-5

1 THESSALONIANS: Living for Jesus *By Julia Marsden*

ISBN: 978-1-906173-67-8

10 Publishing
a division of 10 of those.com

To place an order call: **0844 879 3243** email: **sales@10ofthose.com**
or order online: **www.10ofthose.com**